CREATING Keepsakes

EDITOR-IN-CHIEF Tracy White
SPECIAL PROJECTS EDITOR Leslie Miller
SENIOR EDITOR, SPECIAL PROJECTS Vanessa Hoy
SENIOR WRITER Rachel Thomae
SENIOR EDITOR Lanna Carter
ASSOCIATE WRITER Lori Fairbanks
ASSISTANT EDITOR Britney Mellen
EDITORIAL ASSISTANTS Joannie McBride, Fred Brewer
ART DIRECTOR Brian Tippetts
SPECIAL PROJECTS SENIOR DESIGNER Erin Bayless
DESIGNER Celeste Rockwood-Jones
FOUNDING EDITOR Lisa Bearnson
CO-FOUNDER Don Lambson

PRIMEDIA

VICE PRESIDENT, GROUP PUBLISHER David O'Neil
CIRCULATION MARKETING DIRECTORS Dena Spar, Janice Martin
PROMOTIONS DIRECTOR Dana Smith

PRIMEDIA, Inc.
CHAIRMAN Dean Nelson
PRESIDENT AND CEO Kelly Conlin
VICE-CHAIRMAN Beverly C. Chell

PRIMEDIA Enthusiast Media
EVP, CONSUMER MARKETING/CIRCULATION Steve Aster
SVP, CHIEF FINANCIAL OFFICER Kevin Neary
SVP, MFG., PRODUCTION AND DISTRIBUTION Kevin Mullan
SVP, CHIEF INFORMATION OFFICER Debra C. Robinson
VP, CONSUMER MARKETING Bobbi Gutman
VP, MANUFACTURING Gregory A. Catsaros
VP, SINGLE COPY SALES Thomas L. Fogarty
VP, MANUFACTURING BUDGETS AND OPERATIONS Lilia Golia
VP, HUMAN RESOURCES Kathleen P. Malinowski
VP, BUSINESS DEVELOPMENT Albert Messina
VP, DATABASE /E-COMMERCE Suti Prakash

PRIMEDIA Outdoor Recreation and Enthusiast Group
PRESIDENT Scott Wagner
VP, GROUP CFO Henry Donahue
VP, MARKETING AND INTERNET OPERATIONS Dave Evans

ISBN 1-929180-83-7

©2005, PRIMEDIA, INC.

photographs

I found I could say things with color and shapes that I couldn't say any other way—things I had no words for. —Georgia O'Keefe

be inspired by Leslie Miller

I've never been an "artist." In fact, I grew up thinking that I had absolutely no artistic talent. Even the mere idea of an art class sent me into cold sweats. Maybe it was that fear that made me admire art and artists so much. I love wandering through galleries and museums to see the latest trends as well as the works of the old masters. As an editor in the scrapbook industry, I am constantly amazed by the artistic effects that scrapbookers create on their pages. It was this kind of artistry that inspired this set of books. I wanted to share with you the beauty, the techniques—the art—of these women. And along the way, I discovered that even I, an avowed "non-artist" could try my hand at these artistic techniques. Take for example, Sara Tumpane's "Attitude Adjustment" layout on p. 39. By extending the scene of her photo onto her background, she showed me just how simple—and striking—adding lines of paint to my layout could be. I'm confident as you look through these projects, you'll also find plenty of inspiring ideas to help you find your inner artist!

how to use the
artistic effects book set

Spark your creativity with the *Creating Keepsakes Collection: Artistic Effects* set. Each volume in this five-book set provides a close-up look at the different elements of your scrapbook page and shows you how to reach beyond your scrapbooking supplies to create artistic backgrounds, text elements, photography, embellishments and dimensional projects. We'll show you the steps and ideas behind these artistic pages and projects by translating the designer's artistic techniques with step-by-step instructions as well as easy variations you can try on your own projects with supplies you already own!

With each project, we will show you either:

how to. Visual step-by-steps to walk you through a technique.

variation. Tricks for achieving a similar artistic effect on your page or project.

sidebar. An inspiration checklist for other ideas you can try.

close up. A closer look at how the designer created their page.

A special thank you to our contributing designers: Ali Edwards, Allison Strine, Erin Lincoln, Faye Morrow Bell, Jeniece Higgins, Jen Lessinger, Jenni Bowlin, Joy Bohon, Julie Scattaregia, Kelly Anderson, Lisa Brown Caveney, Loni Stevens, Mellette Berezoski, Pam Kopka, Sara Tumpane and Tracie Smith.

WHAT'S
inside:

>

taking photos to create artistic elements

creative photo backgrounds

To create this page, Faye Morrow Bell used a number of artistic effects. The base of the page is a photograph of a brick wall. Notice how Faye overlaid the wall with a paint-spattered transparency. You can try this artistic effect on your next scrapbook page. Simply start with a photograph and add a painted transparency.

Here are several ideas for photographs that you can take to use as backgrounds:

patterned wallpaper. Look for intricate designs. Make sure to use the zoom lens on your camera to pick up as much detail as you can.

hardwood floors. Look for interesting color striations in the wood. Take photographs at different angles and in various lighting conditions to get a variety of images.

flower gardens and/or fields. Look for bright colors and interesting geometrical arrangements. Look for patterns and lines within the garden itself and then look for interesting detail that you can photograph within each flower.

walkways and paths. Faye used a picture of a brick wall, but you might be able to capture an interesting shot of a brick pathway. Look for texture in concrete as well as mosaic tiles placed on walkways and paths.

fabric. Although you can use fabric directly on your page, don't forget that you can also photograph interesting pieces of fabric and use the photographs themselves as artistic elements.

PEACE: by Faye Morrow Bell
Supplies *Patterned papers:* Carolee's Creations, Design Originals and Flair Designs; *Ribbon:* Making Memories; *Epoxy letters:* Li'l Davis Designs; *Acrylic paint:* Plaid Enterprises; *Crown:* Sonnets, Creative Imaginations; *Phrase:* Pebbles Inc.

DISCOVER NEW YORK: By Jen Lessinger
Supplies *Acrylic paint:* Delta Technical Coatings; *Canvas frame:* Li'l Davis Designs; *Rub-ons:* Making Memories ("discover") and Autumn Leaves ("New York"); *Binder clips:* Office Depot; *Canvas paper:* Fredrix.

(11)

To create the background for her page, Jen printed a photograph of the view of New York City onto canvas. She layered a shot of her husband and son looking down over the photo background. Think about different scenery shots that you can turn into backgrounds for your scrapbook pages.

Want an instant artistic look on your page? Literally frame the subject of your page! Notice how Loni took a picture of herself looking through an empty picture frame.

023249

art·ist (är'tist)
any of the fine
who does anyt
ar·tis·tic (är-tis
2. done skillfu
—ar·tis'ti·cal

a

(är'tist)

live your dreams -- NO EXCUSES

24

THE ARTIST IN ME.

I can tell you, that as an artist & one who has enjoyed the creative process (beginning at a very young age), I don't know what other art form could be more satisfying, or fulfilling, to me personally than scrapbooking is. It's everything I love about art, wrapped up in one! Scrapbooking is also my twist on the concept of journals. I have never been great at keeping a daily journal, so for me, I view my scrapbooks as just that, my journals. I'm preserving those things that are most important to me in my life. My family, traditions, day to day activities, special events, milestones, my beliefs, and my thoughts & feelings in an interesting way for future generations to enjoy. I hope others will be able to pick up on the details of my personality, (even my insecurities) through my artwork as well as my journaling. Many are right there on the surface of my pages. For instance, the fact that I am somewhat of a perfectionist...My love of flowers... My favorite color...lush in green... That I am the daughter of an extremely talented seamstress... My insecurity as a writer (hence the hidden journaling)...And yes, that I probably scrapbook my nieces & nephews way more than their own mothers do; just to name a few! (Can you tell I'm a doting aunt?).

Scrapbooking has changed my life in such a positive way. I view my surroundings & the world I live in a little differently then I did before I became a scrapbooker. I can't flip through a magazine, drive past a billboard, or walk through a store now without taking in the colors, unique designs and feeling inspired by it all. I notice everyday details more closely in things, events & people, which has made me a more insightful person and a better artist. I am so grateful for the role scrapbooking plays in my life. In my wildest dreams, I never imagined I could devote so much time to a passion, or make a living at something I love. Never! It has taught me the importance of discovering & embracing my talents, pursing my passions and doing what makes me happy. As an artist, I am addicted... and way beyond content! Scrapbooking fills that need I have to create. It's something I know I will always enjoy. 11.28.04

THE ARTIST IN ME: by Loni Stevens
Supplies *Patterned Paper*: BasicGrey; *Sheer frame, "Like it Is" sticker, brads and staples*: Making Memories; *Monogram paper ("A") and wood numbers*: Li'l Davis Designs; *Index tab*: 7Gypsies; *Transparency*: Hammermill; *Gesso and antiquing varnish*: Delta Technical Coatings; *Computer fonts*: AL Uncle Charles, downloaded at www.twopeasinabucket.com; Hootie, downloaded from Internet. *Other*: Definitions from dictionary, spiral clip, rhinestones, silk flowers, ticket stub and ribbon.

When taking photographs, you should look for unique viewpoints that will give your photographs a humorous or artistic edge. Notice how Sara captured a unique viewpoint in the photograph of her husband in Washington, D.C. Says Sara, "I saw this perspective, and it was too funny. I got Tim to play along so that I could capture this shot!"

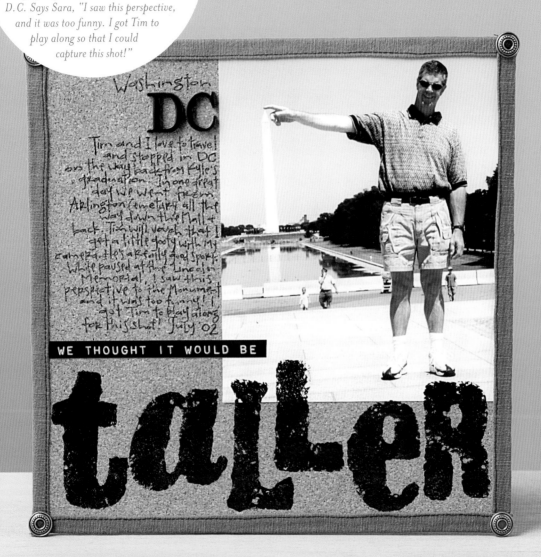

Washington DC

Tim and I love to travel and stopped in DC on the way back from Kyle's graduation. In one great day we went from Arlington Cemetery all the way down the Mall & back. Tim will vouch that I get a little goofy with my camera. He's a really good sport. While paused at the Lincoln Memorial, I saw this perspective to the Monument and it was too funny! I got Tim to play along for this shot! July '02

WE THOUGHT IT WOULD BE

taller

TALLER: by Sara Tumpane
Supplies *Compressed sponges:* Miracle Sponges; *Adhesive cork sheeting:* Duck, Henckel Consumer Adhesives; *Labels:* Dymo; *Wood letters:* Li'l Davis Designs; *Brads:* Making Memories; *Acrylic paint and decoupage medium:* Delta Technical Coatings; *Clear sealer:* Diamond Glaze, JudiKins; *Other:* Fabric.

creative photo accents

Photographs are such an integral part of each layout that you create that it only makes sense to use your photographs as accents on your page as well. On this page, Pam Kopka made mini accents by printing photographs of baby Luke on squares of canvas. Notice how she frayed the canvas squares and attached them to her layout with stickpins.

Consider creating your own photo accents that fit the following themes:

snow. For a winter fun page, consider taking photographs of the snow. For example, a tree with branches heavily laden with snow. Or, snow piled up on the front steps of your porch. Or, a snowman. Resize your image and print onto canvas or a sticker.

cards. For a Valentine's Day page, consider taking pictures of Valentine's Day cards, heart-shaped boxes of candy and/or a Valentine's Day gift. Resize photographs as desired and print them as page embellishments. For an artistic effect, you can print photographs and then modify them by adding paint or glitter.

sand. For a summer page, consider taking pictures of sand, water, close-ups of beach towels, a picnic basket, and more. For an artistic effect, consider gluing actual sand over a picture of the shoreline at the beach.

Remember: When creating a photo accent from your page, you can also use those extra and/or duplicate photographs. Always play with your extra photographs (and be careful when experimenting with originals.)

LUKE: by Pam Kopka
Supplies *Watercolor paper:* Canson; *Patina finish, acrylic paint, gloss and texturing medium:* DecoArt; *Embossing enamel:* Stamping It; *Gesso:* Delta Technical Coatings; *Rubber stamps:* Stampers Anonymous and Creative Block; *Jigsaw letters, molding strip and stickpin:* Making Memories; *Embossing enamel:* Suze Weinberg; *Mesh:* Magic Mesh.

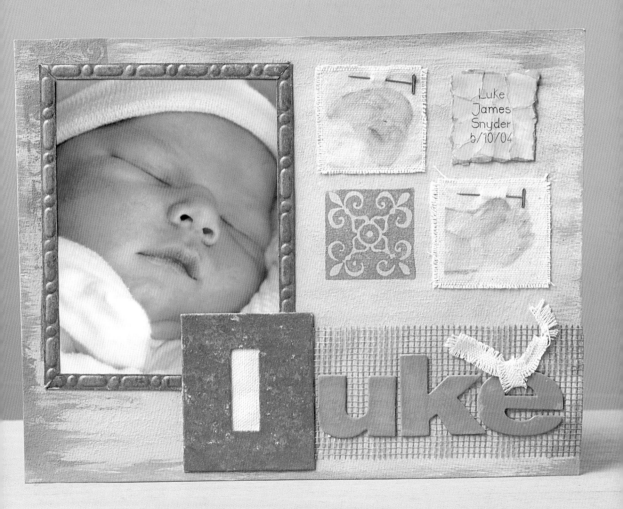

Luke
James
Snyder
6/10/04

Luke

MERRY LITTLE CHRISTMAS: by Ali Edwards
Supplies *Textured cardstock:* Bazzill Basics Paper; *Patterned paper:* Flair Designs; *Punch and corner rounder:* Marvy Uchida; *Ribbon:* May Arts; *Letter stamps:* Ma Vinci's Reliquary; *Rub-ons:* Making Memories; *"Memories" accent:* KI Memories; *Other:* Canvas and staples.

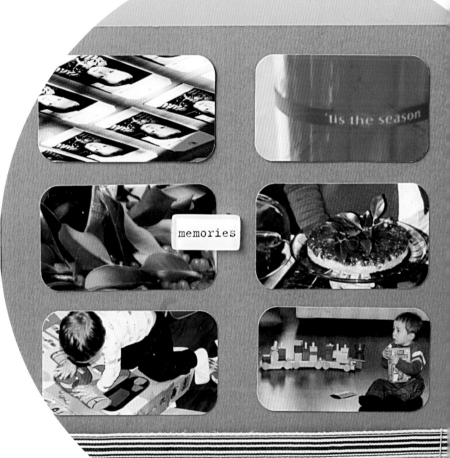

'tis the season

memories

urself a

When you take pictures, look for the "big picture" as well as details that capture your feelings and impressions of a special event. Notice the unique viewpoints captured in Ali's photographs on this page.

2

image transfer & creative photo printing

more ideas with photos

To create the lovely look on her page, Mellette used a photo-editing program to size and change the picture of her daughter to black and while. She then printed the photo onto iron-on film. She cut out the photograph and ironed it onto fabric according to the manufacturer's instructions. Finally, she trimmed the fabric and machine-stitched it to the layout.

For an alternative, you could also print your photograph directly onto canvas. However, the advantage of using an iron-on transfer is that if you wished, you could transfer to a range of different fabrics that would accept the image in different ways. Imagine ironing your image onto lace or even onto a nubby and/or textured fabric. Or, what about ironing an image onto a piece of fabric that had a very light print or pattern to it?

Note: Look at the pretty silk flowers that Mellette used as accents on her page. She bought silk flowers and then edged the petals with two coats of gold leafing pen. She painted the buttons with gold leafing pen and attached the buttons to the inside of the flowers.

GRACE WAS IN ALL HER STEPS: by Mellette Berezoski
Supplies *Patterned papers:* Chatterbox, BasicGrey, and Daisy D's Paper Co.; *Gold leafing pen:* Krylon; *Paper tag:* BasicGrey; *Vellum quote:* Memories Complete; *Iron-on film:* Avery; *Heart brad:* Magic Scraps; *Ribbon, eyelets and staples:* Making Memories; *Adhesive:* Glue Dots International; *Other:* Silk flowers, fabric and buttons.

maysie
aug. '04

grace was in all her steps.
heaven in her eye.

– John Milton

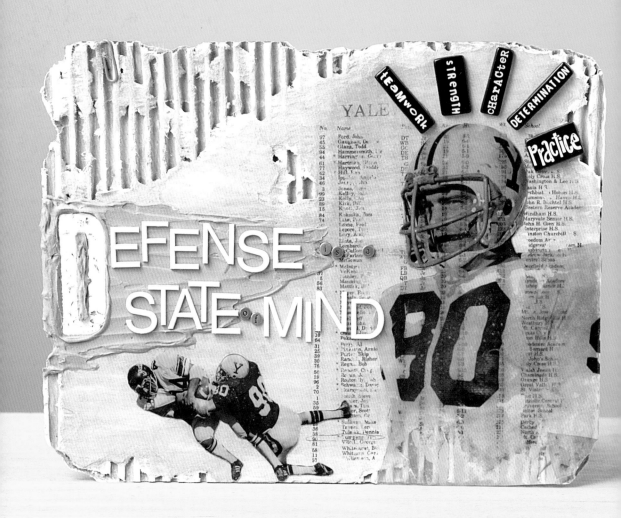

DEFENSE IS A STATE OF MIND: by Sara Tumpane
Supplies *Dimensional and acrylic paint:* Delta Technical Coatings; *Foam stamp and letter charms:* Making Memories; *Clay words:* Li'l Davis Designs; *Plastic letters:* Quartet; *Transfer media:* Artisan's Choice and Golden Artist Colors; *Transfer adhesive:* Golden Artist Colors.

Photo Image Transfer

There are all kinds of ways to transfer photographs to elements on your pages. To create this page, Sara used a glossy gel transfer medium. Says Sara, "To create the look on this page, I applied gel medium to the area of my page where I wanted the image to transfer. I placed a reversed copy of my image over the gel and burnished it with a bone folder. Then, I gently pulled the paper off, leaving the transferred image on my background."

There are many ways to transfer images, including packing tape transfer and other alternatives. To read more about image transfer, see the step-by-step on page 31.

Tip:
Looking for a cool image to transfer to your page? Don't have the exact image that you need? Go to the Internet and search for an image that will match the theme of your page. Click on the image and save it to your computer. Import the image into your photo-editing program and make any desired changes. Print the image and transfer it to your project.

ocean **Discover**)(**Carnival** mexico

Mexico

ESCAPE **BEACH** mexico VACATION **Cruise Ship**

Knutson family Christmas cruise 1996 ✻ key west, FL.
✻ cozumel, mexico ✻ playa del carmen ✻ m...

MEXICO: by Kelly Anderson
Supplies *Textured paper:* Creative Imaginations; *Transfer medium:* Liquid Sculpey, Polyform Products; *Rubber stamps:* PSX Designs; *Stamping ink:* Brilliance, Tsukineko; *Pen:* Zig Millennium, EK Success; *Other:* Magazine clippings.

*Kelly transferred images
from a travel brochure onto
Liquid Sculpey to create the unique
page accent at the top of her page. You
can transfer photographs onto liquid
sculpey as well. To learn other methods of
image transfer, see pages 23 and 31!*

Tracie started with a cropped photo then distressed the edges by sanding them to create a border and stitched a partial border onto the photo using hemp and a straight stitch. "I used acrylic paint to alter the self-adhesive moulding strips and then adhered them to the page to create a border," she adds. Her secret to printing the journaling on canvas? "I printed on typing paper first, used spray adhesive to adhere the canvas to the typing paper and then ran it back through my printer," she shares. Then, she stitched the journaling blocks to the page using a sewing machine.

I think it is imp... outlet for self-exp... become scrapbook... when I am creating... though sometimes it... way that I imagined it... about scrapbooking to... photography has greatly i... beginning to scrapbook four year... photo is worth a thousand words, so i... continue to improve in this area.

I usually listen to No Doubt while I create. One of the highlights of this past year was getting backstage passes for their concert. We ended up in the 8th row and I felt like I was part of the band that night. They were rockin!

Tracie SMITH

Some of my best inspiration comes to me right before I doze off to sleep.

I call my husband, Jaime, the "Simon Cowell" of scrapbooking. He always gives me his honest opinion even if he knows it's not what I want to hear. When he gives me the thumbs up on a layout, I know I've created a winner. His opinion means the world to me.

My two boys keep me young at heart even though they give me tons of gray hair! My oldest, Justin, loves to play games. Our favorite is Monopoly Jr. Harrison is so loving and sweet to me. He plays with my hair constantly. I was most concerned about his opinion when I recently dyed it red. It was a shock to my family, but it's growing on me for sure! Oh, and he still twirls it even though it's red.

TRACIE: by Tracie Smith
Supplies *Patterned paper:* BasicGrey; *Acrylic paint, molding, jigsaw letter and brads:* Making Memories; *Buttons:* Hero Arts; *Hemp:* Stampin' Up!; *Labels:* Dymo; *Heart button:* K&Company; *Pen:* Zig Millennium, EK Success; *Other:* Canvas and silk flowers.

OLIVIA: by Allison Strine

Supplies *Rubber stamps:* Creative Imaginations ("Younique") and Stampers Anonymous (stitches); *Stamping ink:* Magic Mica, Clearsnap; *Polymer clay:* Prēmo Translucent Liquid Sculpey, Polyform Products; *Acrylic paint:* DecoArt; *Bookbinding tape and ribbon:* Making Memories; *Other:* Rug, canvas, wax linen and letters.

Allison transferred this picture of her daughter to clay. Notice how she added eyelets to the clay before baking it in her oven. After the image had cooled and dried, Allison was able to thread string through the eyelets to create an accent on her page.

photograph puzzles

It's fun to play with your photographs! Another way to create an artistic effect with your photographs is to transfer them to a dimensional surface (for example, on this page, Sara transferred photographs to heavy chipboard) and then use a scroll saw to cut the chipboard into pieces. You can cut them into basic shapes, like squares, or you can make them into a puzzle to feature on your page.

Here's an easy way that you can transfer photographs to a surface such as chipboard:

- Make copies of your photographs. Print them on plain paper or cardstock.
- Apply decoupage medium to the back of the photographs.
- Attach photographs to chipboard.
- Apply a layer of decoupage medium over the top of photographs.
- Cut the photographs into desired pieces.
- Paint acrylic paint along the edge of each piece.
- Sand the edge of each piece.
- Attach the pieces to your layout.

note: Decoupaged puzzle pieces may not be safe to give to a young child who might put them in his or her mouth. Otherwise, you should be fine creating your own traditional puzzle.

fun idea: If you have old scrapbooking templates for cutting photographs, consider using the templates as the base for your puzzle design. Lighter weights of chipboard can be cut with a scissors or even a craft knife.

You can also use image transfer techniques to transfer photographs to chipboard. For more information on how to do image transfer, see page 31!

YALE BULLDOGS: by Sara Tumpane
Supplies *Color wash dye:* Ranger Industries; *Watercolor paper:* Strathmore Artist Papers; *Clear gloss:* Delta Technical Coatings; *Epoxy numbers and frames:* Li'l Davis Designs; *Letter rub-ons:* Making Memories and Li'l Davis Designs; *White ink:* Spectralite, Dr. Ph. Martin's, Salis International Inc.; *Pen:* Zig Millennium, EK Success; *Other:* Chipboard.

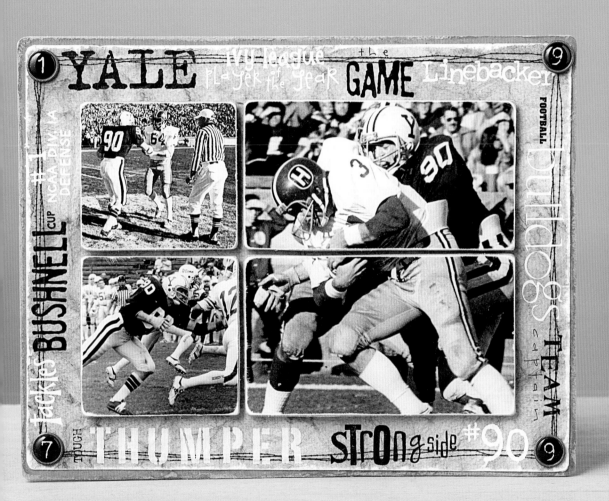

YALE — IVY LEAGUE Player of the Year — the GAME — Linebacker

① ⑨

tackles — #1 — BUSHNELL CUP — NCAA DIV IA DEFENSE

FOOTBALL

Bulldogs TEAM captain

TOUGH THUMPER — STRONg side #90

⑦ ⑨

REMEMBER THE GIRL: by Allison Strine
Supplies *Transfer paper:* Lazertran; *Transparency and eyelets:* Creative Imaginations; *Rose image:* Hampton Art Stamps; *Calligraphy ink:* Dr. Ph. Martin's, Salis International Inc.; *Polymer clay:* Prēmo Sculpey, Polyform Products; *Brass mesh:* Anima Designs; *Color wash dyes:* Ranger Industries; *Other:* Beeswax, buttons, canvas and magazine clippings.

how to transfer an image onto clay:

STEP 1: Print or photocopy an image in reverse onto photo transfer paper. Condition and roll out polymer clay to the same size as image.

STEP 2: Cut out image and press onto clay, image-side down.

STEP 3: Float clay in water until backing paper slides off and bake clay as directed.

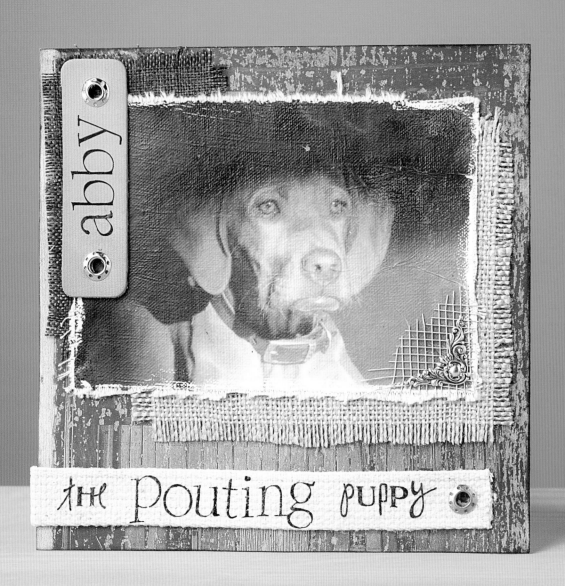

THE POUTING PUPPY: by Julie Scattaregia
Supplies *Patterned paper:* The Paper Loft; *Rub-ons:* Li'l Davis Designs and Making Memories; *Transfer:* Lazertran; *Fabric and eyelets:* Creative Imaginations; *Metal screen and letters:* Making Memories; *Leather:* Rusty Pickle; *Other:* Burlap, canvas and twill.

Image Transfer with Transfer Paper

Looking for another way to transfer photographs to canvas? You know that you can print photographs directly onto canvas and that you can print photographs onto iron-on transfer paper and iron them onto canvas.

Here's another variation from Julie Scattaregia using transfer paper. Follow these easy steps to achieve the look that she presents on "The Pouting Puppy" layout.

1. *Using a color copier, photocopy image to the transfer paper. (Follow the manufacturer's instructions regarding the use of a color copier or ink-jet printer.)*

2. *Brush a piece of canvas fabric with gel medium. Allow the gel to completely dry.*

3. *Trim the photo image to size. Soak the image in water for several minutes.*

4. *Carefully remove the paper backing from the image.*

5. *Place the image on the prepared canvas.*

6. *Allow the image to dry overnight.*

NORTH CAROLINA OUTER BANKS: by Allison Strine
Supplies *Patterned paper and metal accent:* Li'l Davis Designs; *Iron-on transfer paper:* Hewlett-Packard; *Acrylic paint:* DecoArt; *Rub-ons:* Scrapperware, Creative Imaginations; *Other:* Canvas, fabric, beads, buttons and label.

Allison used iron-on film to transfer the images to the front of her cloth-covered album. Notice how she created visual interest by attaching all sorts of unique objects to the photograph of her daughter: a piece of blue rope, a label, tiny rock beads, fibers and ribbons. On the inner pages of the album, Allison printed and sewed her photos directly onto the album pages. Then, she overlaid the images with pieces of cork, faux labels, ripped pieces of paper and transparencies.

BEACH

does the
song of the
Sea
end at the
shore or in
the hearts
of those who
listen to it

creative photo placement

The first time someone called me an artist I probably laughed. Who me? Artists live in New York. They paint and draw and sing and live fabulously abstract lives and drink lots of coffee. OK, well, I have the coffee part down to a science. And yet, I am an artist. I work with my hands. And my head. And my heart. I use my imagination. I tell stories through words, photos and precious little accents. Some days I live in the past. Consumed by memories. An effort to remember and bring a story to life. Other days I live in the present. Recording moments through art. Living a creative life. An artist's life. My life. Imagine that...

"July: the greatest gift you have to give is that of your own self-transformation."
— Katen
it's the simple things

A...EVERYDAY: by Ali Edwards
Supplies *Cardstock:* Bazzill Basics Paper; *Patterned papers:* Fiddlerz3, Memory Box, 7gypsies, Waste Not; *Computer fonts:* Baskerville, Verdana; *Pen:* American Crafts; *Rub-ons:* Li'l Davis Designs (numbers), Wordsworth (phrase); *Other:* Staples and ribbon.

A design tip from Ali? Size your photograph to match your journaling block to create a page with instant eye-appeal! Notice how Ali repeated the circle accent on both her photograph and journaling block.

To create the background on her page, Sara printed her photograph onto canvas paper then hand-painted the background, extending the image from the photograph onto the canvas background of her page. Even if you don't consider yourself an artist, you can still copy Sara's technique by choosing one or two prominent colors from your photograph and applying simple strips of paint across your page background.

ATTITUDE ADJUSTMENT: by Sara Tumpane
Supplies *Primed art canvas and inkjet canvas photo paper:* Fredrix; *Chipboard letters:* Li'l Davis Designs; *Acrylic paint:* Delta Technical Coatings; *Paint thickener:* Liquitex; *Pen:* Sharpie; *Glue dots:* Glue Dots International; *Other:* Flowers from a hair barrette.

creative ways to display photographs on your page

To create this beautiful page background, Jeniece stamped her title with resistance ink and embossed the images with clear embossing powder. She applied watercolors over the stamped images and then used a tissue to rub away excess paint.

Notice her creative method of displaying the photograph. By sewing loops of ribbon across the top of her photograph, she was able to hang her photo from a mini-dowel rod on her page. The photograph actually lifts up to reveal journaling about her daughter's love of rain and rainbows.

RAINBOW SEEKER: by Jeniece Higgins
Supplies *Rubber stamps:* Ma Vinci's Reliquary; *Stamping ink:* VersaMark, Tsukineko; *Embossing powder:* USArtQuest; *Watercolor paint:* Loew-Cornell; *Epoxy letters:* Creative Imaginations; *Rub-ons and corner stamp:* Making Memories; *Watercolor paper:* Canson; *Ribbon:* C.M. Offray & Son; *Embroidery floss:* DMC; *Buttons:* Dress It Up, Jesse James & Co.; *Other:* Thread, dowel and ticket.

Mikaela loves to play in the rain! As soon as she notices it starting, she is quick to grab an umbrella and head out. She is always convinced there will be a rainbow on this particular day we didn't see one at first. Mikaela was happy splashing in the puddles, lifting her open mouth to the sky for a drink, and spinning her umbrella. When the rainbow finally began to shine through, Mikaela was the first to notice it. Of course, we had to run down the block in search of the pot of gold!

DORK: by Erin Lincoln
Supplies *Patterned papers:* KI Memories and Arctic Frog; *Tag card, rubber stamps, stickers, bookbinding tape and rub-ons:* Making Memories; *Bottle caps:* Li'l Davis Designs; *Concho:* Scrapworks; *Computer font:* CK Chemistry, "Fresh Fonts" CD, *Creating Keepsakes; Other:* Buttons, ribbon and floss.

SHE'S ALL THAT

Going overboard wild

Get the inside scoop

YOU CAN'T MAKE THIS STUFF UP!
TWO HONEST PICTURES, BOTH OF
ELIZABETH BEING GOOFY!

Looking for a way to add more photographs to your page? Think about creating artistic photo pockets and about displaying photographs on tags.

5K race

goofing off

FIGHT!

water

I GUESS THEY GOT SO BORED WITH RUNNING WITH THE RESIDENT SLOWPOKE (ME!) THAT THEY DECIDED TO MAKE SOME FUN OF THEIR OWN. AT ONE POINT, LIZ WAS RUNNING AWAY FROM THE FINISH LINE TO DRENCH DANNY...SILLY KIDS! JULY 3, 2004

you better run

Using a ruler, line up graphic tape to frame photos or words.

5K RACE: by Erin Lincoln
Supplies *Patterned paper:* Daisy D's Paper Co.; *Transparency:* K&Company; *Stamping ink:* ColorBox, Clearsnap; *Rubber stamps, acrylic paint and metal letters:* Making Memories; *Conchos:* Scrapworks; *Graphic tape:* Headline.

For a new way to crop photos, create a free form line across the bottom of a photo with graphic tape. Trim the photo just below the tape line.

simons iSLanD

ST. SIMON'S ISLAND: by Lisa Brown Caveney
Supplies *Graphic tape:* Chartpak; *Letter stickers:* BasicGrey; *Pen:* Zig Writer, EK Success; *Other:* Cork.

Graphic Tape

Graphic tape is a thin tape that comes in different colors. It's very easy to use this tape to create a variety of different artistic effects on your pages.

(left) For example, Erin used graphic tape to frame her photographs and to set off the words under the photographs. (above) Lisa, on the other hand, used it to create a free-form line across the bottom of her photograph. Her advice: "Make sure not to touch the focal point of your photograph when using this technique." After placing the tape, Lisa trimmed her photograph just below the free-form line.

REMEMBER YOU ARE NOT PERFECT: by Pam Kopka
Supplies *Color wash dyes and embossing ink:* Ranger Industries; *Acrylic paint, gloss and glaze spray:* DecoArt; *Embossing enamel:* Stamp It; *Gel medium:* Liquitex; *Photo coloring pens:* Spot Pen; *Watercolor paper:* Canson; *Transparencies:* Magic Scraps; *Pen:* American Crafts; *Staples:* Making Memories; *Lettering:* Clearly Yours, K&Company; *Clip art:* Dover Publications; *Rubber stamps:* Stampers Anonymous (border) and unknown (flower); *Other:* Twill tape.

Pam wanted to create a
layout that told a story about
herself as an artist. She manipulated
her photograph in a photo-editing program (notice how she deepened the hue of
her green eyes.) She cut her photographs
into squares and placed wire over each
image. She then put the pieces back
together again to create the look
of an artistic puzzle.

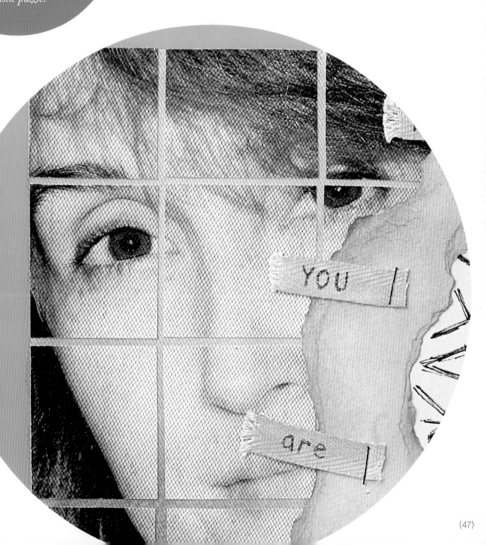

AN ARTIST? IS THAT WHAT YOU CALL IT? HMMMM. NOT SURE I AGREE WITH THAT. I'M A PAPER CUTTER.

I am shaped by my experiences

I AM SHAPED BY MY EXPERIENCES: **by Erin Lincoln**
Supplies *Patterned paper*: Anna Griffith, NRN Designs, Paper Fever; *Rub-ons and brad*: Making Memories; *Computer font*: CK Chemistry, "Fresh Fonts" CD, *Creating Keepsakes*, Piranesi Lt BT, Corel Systems; *Pen*: Pigment Pro, American Crafts; *Stitching template*: Li'l Davis Designs; *Other*: Floss.

Notice how Erin made her color photograph stand out by grouping it with a block of black and white photographs.

MELLETTE ♥ BEREZOSKI

The position of the *artist* is humble. He is essentially a *channel.*

-Piet Mondrian

CREATE
Art is one's own instrument of expression.
LOVE
An artist finds joy in the process, in the exploration as well as in the discovery.
NURTURE
Creativity is allowing yourself to make mistakes.
GIVE
Every work of art is a masterpiece if it originates in the heart.

MELLETTE BEREZOSKI: by Mellette Berezoski
Supplies *Patterned paper:* Autumn Leaves; *Transparency:* Hammermill; *Brads:* Making Memories; *Computer fonts:* Times New Roman and Rage Italic, Microsoft Word; AL Worn Machine, Autumn Leaves Font CD; *Other:* Silk flower and thread.

creative photo placement

On this page, Ali used a large photograph as a background element. Notice how she positioned the large formal photograph as a muted background (to achieve the muted effect on the large formal photograph, she layered a transparency over the top of it. You can achieve a similar effect by layering vellum over a photograph). Her journaling box, however, is anything but formal. She used candid fun photographs of herself and her husband to decorate the cover of her journaling matchbook and decorated the book with phrases such as "excitement," "anticipation" and "fun."

You can juxtapose photographs, formal and candid, to create artistic looks on your scrapbook pages. Here are a few ideas on fun ways to "mix it up" on your scrapbook pages!

Start with a formal graduation picture, such as a senior picture taken by a professional photographer. Now, add candid photographs of friends goofing around together and smiling big for the camera.
Start with a professional photograph of your child, such a posed picture of your child taken at a photo studio. Now, add candid photographs of your child experiencing a range of moods and/or imperfect moments (for example, food on her face, messy hair or a mismatched outfit).
Have a headshot from the place where you work? Start with your posed "business" shot and add fun pictures of yourself that show what you like to do during your free time.
Have a formal family photograph? Juxtapose it with photographs of each family member acting silly or just doing something that he or she loves to do.

BECOMING EDWARDS: by Ali Edwards
Supplies *Textured cardstock:* Bazzill Basics Paper; *Patterned papers:* Daisy D's Paper Co. and Anna Griffin; *Patterned transparency:* 7gypsies; *Metal tags, matchbook card and white tag:* Making Memories; *Dimensional adhesive:* Diamond Glaze, JudiKins; *Letter stamps:* PSX Designs and Ma Vinci's Reliquary; *"E" accent:* Li'l Davis Designs; *Negative strip:* Narratives, Creative Imaginations; *Pen:* American Crafts.

love

the beginning

(bEcomiNg edWarDs)

the anticipation ... the excitement ... the

august 98 first

and

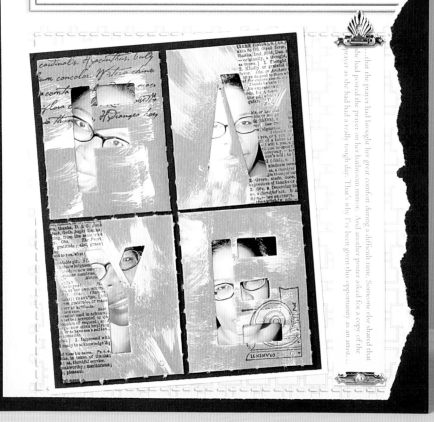

EVENT: CK Art Book - Biography

PARTICIPANTS: Faye Morrow Bell

COMMENTS: I never imagined myself an artist. But author Marianne Williamson reminds us that *"No matter what form our job or activity takes, the content is the same as everyone else's: we are here to minister to human hearts".* I've received more accolades than imaginable as a scrapbook artist…and I am grateful for each and every one. But the greatest compliment was one I stumbled across on a message board. I love Marjorie Holmes' prayer for a daily dose of grace — and I included it in my book. Someone posted…

…that the prayer had brought her great comfort during a difficult time. Someone else shared that she had posted the prayer on her bathroom mirror. And another poster asked for a copy of the prayer as she had had a really tough day. That's why I've been given this opportunity as an artist…

CK ART BOOK - BIOGRAPHY : by Faye Morrow Bell
Supplies *Cardstock*: Bazzill Basics Paper; *Patterned paper*: K&Company; *Rubber stamps*: Stampin' Up! and Hero Arts; *Ink*: Stampin' Up!; *Stencil letters*: U.S. Stamp and Sign; *Computer fonts*: Centaur and Times New Roman; *Paint*: Delta Technical Coatings; *Other*: Hinge.

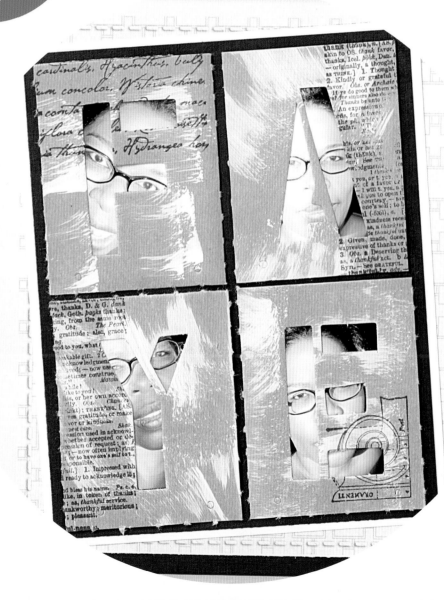

Trim an 11" x 14" matte board frame to border an 8½" x 11" layout.

Creative Photo Splicing

There are a variety of ways to present photographs on your page that go beyond the traditional photo mat for a 4" x 6" or 3½" x 5" photograph. On this page, Joy Bohon enlarged photographs of her daughter and sliced them into long vertical rectangles. She also attached the photographs inside a precut matte board frame. She distressed the frame by sanding it and then applied a coat of dimensional glaze to add extra visual interest.

Think about these creative ways to splice your photographs (as always, take care when cutting your photographs. Make sure that you don't cut away important detail and/or splice into your focal point.)

• Cut a photograph into horizontal strips and stack the strips on top of each other.

• Cut two photographs into squares. Piece photographs back together as a whole unit—or experiment by replacing pieces of one photograph with another photograph.

• Take a ruler and draw diagonal lines across the back of your photograph. Use a craft knife to carefully slice the photograph into sections. Glue the sections back together on your scrapbook page.

defeat (de·fet) 1. ... victory over 2. fall at the hand of a rival   teamwork   practice   succe

... expectation successfully 2 ... obtain or reach what one set out to do   team

A5710367401235

92348757

mmitment (ke·mit·men) 1. to dedicate oneself to something or someone 2. duty promise   sportsman

[**com·mit·ment**
TO DEDICATE ONESELF TO SOMETHING OR SOMEONE]

Athlete   **PEARL**
I AM PROUD

SHE'S ALL THAT

ATHLETE: by Joy Bohon
Supplies *Patterned paper and transparency:* Art Warehouse, Creative Imaginations; *Definition and word stickers:* Making Memories; *Epoxy letters:* Shotz, Creative Imaginations; *Bookplate:* Li'l Davis Designs; *Rubber stamp:* Art Warehouse for Limited Edition Rubberstamps; *Stamping ink:* StazOn, Tsukineko; *Labels:* Dymo; *Brads:* Lost Art Treasures; *Dimensional adhesive:* Diamond Glaze, JudiKins; *Other:* Twill and matte board.

altered photographs

like any artist, i love my creative time.
there is no activity that captivates me quite
like art does. In my world, bliss is getting down
& dirty in a mess of paint, textured papers,
stamps...anything interesting! A creative mess
is always preferable to idle neatness.

my one rule about art: there are no mistakes
in the process of creating, only lessons. most
inventions & innovations are the result of
so-called accidents. Have fun!

KELLY: by Kelly Anderson
Supplies *Cardstock*: Memory Lane; *Foam stamp and acrylic paint*: Making Memories; *White pen*: Gelly Roll; *Transparency*: C-Line Products.

like any artist, i love my creative time.
no activity that captivates me
my world, bliss

placing accents on photographs

Do you see the large letter "A" positioned in the bottom left hand corner of Ali's layout? Believe it or not, it's a photograph that she took to use as a page accents! Look at Ali's pages, and you'll find photographs used as accents—and you'll find that she creates artistic effects by placing accents directly on her photographs.

Don't be afraid to modify your photographs and create an artistic effect in any of the following ways. (Editor's note: Remember, use duplicate photographs when experimenting with art techniques on your photos!)

take acrylic paint and brush it along the edges of photographs. Alternative: Swipe acrylic paint on the edges of a transparency and layer the transparency over the photo.

rubber stamp directly on photographs and/or on copies of photographs. Don't forget that you can emboss on photographs as well.

use double-sided tape along edges of photographs. Sprinkle tiny beads or glitter along tape and use it to create an artistic photo frame.

remember, use care when modifying photographs. You want to create an artistic look that is pleasing to the eye—but you don't want to draw attention away from the subject of your photograph or the story that you want to tell.

THINGS THAT BRING ME JOY: by Ali Edwards
Supplies *Patterned papers:* KI Memories (stripe), Anna Griffin (herringbone), Paper Adventures (pink floral) and Chatterbox (pale pink); *Rectangle accents:* KI Memories; *Rub-on phrases:* Wordsworth; *Rub-on letters:* Creative Imaginations (white) and Li'l Davis Designs (black); *Hinges, acrylic paint and "S" accent:* Making Memories; *Index card:* Autumn Leaves; *Modeling paste:* Liquitex; *Pen:* American Crafts.

moments

together

it's the simple things

kisses

ART

your sweet gaze.

A

time with you

you bless me

time just for me

JOYFUL

THINGS that BRING me JOY

OPEN

delight in the ordinary

The expression on your face says it all. You finished your First Holy Communion. After all the struggles to get you to class and to do your homework – you finally made it!

YOU FINALLY MADE IT!: by Pam Kopka
Supplies *Watercolor paper:* Canson; *Stencil and tea dye varnish:* Delta Technical Coatings; *Acrylic paints:* DecoArt; *Stucco paste:* Liquitex; *Acrylic sealer:* Krylon; *Computer font:* Unknown.

how to create a "peeled paint" look on a photo:

STEP 1: Apply a coat of decoupage medium over areas on your layout you want to remain visible (such as a photo). Spread a thin layer of petroleum jelly over the decoupaged area. The petroleum jelly prevents the paint from adhering to your layout and photo, and will wipe away without leaving a residue.

STEP 2: Paint entire layout with acrylic paint. Let dry.

STEP 3: Rub petroleum jelly from layout with a paper towel.

Five nights in Moorea. This was the view from our beach side hut. It was a beautiful way to celebrate 10 years together.

2004

Perfection

MOOREA
PEARL RESORT

MOOREA PEARL RESORT: by Tracie Smith
Supplies *Hemp paper:* Creative Imaginations; *Mica:* Moon Rose; *Decal paper:* Lazertran; *Stitching template:* Li'l Davis Designs; *Foam core:* Hunt; *Walnut ink:* Postmodern Design; *Rub-on word and date stamp:* Making Memories; *Shipping tag:* Avery; *Dimensional adhesive:* Diamond Glaze, JudiKins; *Pen:* American Crafts; *Other:* Hemp and ephemera.

Clear Effects with Photos

To create the beautiful artistic effect with her photograph, Tracie printed it onto a transparency and then layered thin sheets of mica over the photograph. To adhere the mica, she used a clear-drying dimensional glaze. Notice how the mica and transparency combine to create a magical look of the island where Tracie and her husband celebrated their ten-year anniversary.

There are many different things that you can layer over your photographs to create special effects. (Editor's note: Remember, use duplicate photographs when experimenting with art techniques on your photos!)

Here are just a few variations that you can try:
- Brush dimensional glaze directly over the photo.
- Layer an altered transparency over the photo.
- Place clear page pebbles or clear dimensional stickers over portions of your photograph.
- Place microscope slides over portions of your photo.

Five nigh in Moore. This was the view from our beach side hut. It was a beautiful way to celebrate 10 years together.

PERFECTION

Sara printed her photograph onto ink-jet shrink film and then baked it in the oven to reduce the size. Sara notes, "you will have to print the photo at 8.5" x 11" to get an end result of the size featured on my layout." To learn more about creating page accents with shrink film, see page 66 in the Artistic Effects for Embellishments book!

it. Quiet
shing by.
ant. I can
want. Up
the runs
autiful...
on skis.

park city

FREEDOM on skis

ON SKIS

There is nothing quite like it. Quiet
and cold. Air rushing by.
I can go anywhere I want. I can
go as fast as I want. Up
in the mountains where the runs
are long and beautiful...
cruising...FREEDOM on skis.

2004

S

park city

FREEDOM ON SKIS: by Sara Tumpane

Supplies *Inkjet shrink film:* Grafix; *Acrylic paint:* Delta Technical Coatings; *Wood letters:* Li'l Davis Designs; *Leather:* Tandy; *Iron-on film:* Epson; *Snowflakes:* Center Street Designs; *Letter tag:* The Card Connection; *Letter snaps:* Turtle Press; *Computer fonts:* Playbill, downloaded from www.myfonts.com; Arial Rounded, Microsoft Word; *Other:* Jump rings and clothes snaps.

color wash your photo

In this book, you've seen photographs printed on canvas. You've also seen photographs ironed onto canvas. But on this page, Sara takes a photo on canvas to the next level. Notice how she printed her black-and-white photo on canvas and then used a color wash to add color to the bottom of her photograph (reminiscent of water on the shoreline of the beach).

To make an easy color wash, you can simply mix ink from a re-inker or acrylic paint with a small amount of water. Just brush the mixed color over the portion of your canvas photograph where you want the color to be. You can get a variety of different effects based on the amount of paint that you use to color your canvas. Also, different weights and textures of canvas will accept paint differently, so take this into consideration when experimenting with this technique.

Here are some ideas for photographs to color-enhance with washes. To maximize the effect of your photograph, use a photo-editing program to change it to black and white first and then print onto canvas.

flowers. Print in black and white and then color wash a single flower.
landscape photographs. Color wash a single element that you want to highlight. For example, color wash a beautiful mountain range or sandstone formation.
group shots. Want to create a page that focuses on a single person in the shot? Color wash your grandmother's dress or your son's striped shirt.

YOUNG AT HEART: by Sara Tumpane
Supplies *Iron-on transfer film:* Epson; *Paperclay:* Creative Paperclay; *Acrylic paint and clear sealer:* Delta Technical Coatings; *Stamping ink:* Ranger Industries and 7gypsies; *Metal-rimmed tags and rub-ons:* Making Memories; *Other:* Natural art canvas, chipboard and jute.

not so little anymore, but still

yOUNg at hEARt

june '02

Clayton and Brian

MINE: by Jenni Bowlin
Supplies *Canvas art paper:* Strathmore Artist Papers; *Metal bookplate and letter stickers:* Li'l Davis Designs; *Acrylic paint:* Delta Technical Coatings; *Ribbon:* May Arts.

how to color a black-and-white canvas photo:

STEP 1:   Print a black-and-white photo onto canvas paper.

STEP 2:   Paint sections of the photo using a mixture of acrylic paint and water.

v

using scraps on your pages

To create this page, Jen printed the photograph of her son on art canvas. She used a straight edge to rip the edges of the photograph. After positioning the photo on her page, she found herself thinking of ways that she could use the leftover scraps of art canvas. She took the extra pieces, ripped them into strips and used one strip as a bow (attached to the photo anchor on her page). She used the other strip as a border across the bottom of her page (notice how the strip meets her title and extends it across her page).

You can use your scraps in many artistic ways. In fact, using scraps is a great way to get your feet wet if you are hesitant about trying a new technique! Why not use your scraps in one of these creative ways?

ribbon scraps.
Tie small bits of ribbon to a metal ring to create a beribboned accent for your page. Or, punch holes in the side of your cardstock and tie small ribbons through the holes.

paper scraps.
Paint, splatter or spray a variety of colors and textures of paint onto strips of cardstock or leftover paper. Experiment by tearing papers to find out how different papers rip. Take painted pieces and layer together to form collaged borders, background or accent pieces.

photo scraps.
Trimming your photographs? Take the leftover pieces and coat them with an adhesive. Sprinkle fine beads or glitter on the strips and allow them to dry. Randomly attach these strips to a piece of background cardstock to create an artistic effect.

MY BABY: by Jen Lessinger
Supplies *Photo turn:* 7gypsies; *Canvas paper:* Fredrix; *Heart punch:* EK Success; *Brad:* Creative Imaginations; *Computer fonts:* Dirty Ego, downloaded from the Internet; Century Gothic, Microsoft Word.

♥ MY BABY

You are not really a baby anymore, Bean. You can dress yourself. You brush your teeth and pick out your clothes. You assert your independence regularly - "I can do it!" But there are still moments like this, when I catch you on the couch with your thumb in your mouth. Those sweet soft little cheeks ... those green eyes, so like mine and Daddy's ... that little boy nose. Yes, you are almost four. But you are still

Sara created this page to make a state-
ment about art. For an artistic effect, she
coated the entire image with dimensional
glaze. After the glaze dried, she cracked the
glaze. Sara explains: "I thought it would
be a great way to show that art is imperfect
and that it's okay to have a few
cracks showing. Art is freedom to
do whatever you want.
No rules!"

take a look around you and you'll see it...

in every day life
on TV and in print,
in the eyes of loved
ones + in nature.
Art, manmade and
imperfect, or exqui-
sitely made by the
Master Artist. It's free
flowing + free form.
Anything does + that's
what I love about it!
No rules... I can do
anything. Its the
perfect way to make
my pages + memories
UNIQUE. The ultimate
freedom. I'm here
on Wai'anapanapa
Beach... a speci-
tacular painting
on nature's can-
vas. Look around
you...

enjoy the
Journey

ART is everywhere

ART IS EVERYWHERE: by Sara Tumpane
Supplies *Chipboard phrase, leather photo corners and clay letters*: Li'l Davis Designs; *Acrylic paint, clear gloss varnish and texture medium*: Delta
Technical Coatings; *Metal letter/numbers*: Making Memories; *Dimensional glaze*: Diamond Glaze, JudiKins; *Permanent pen*: Sharpie; *Other*:
Chipboard and ric rac.

Photo Effects on Canvas

As you've noticed throughout this book, you can achieve many different looks by printing your photographs onto canvas art paper. To take this idea one step further, think about different things you can do to alter the printed canvas. For example, on this page, the designer stamped directly on top of the canvas print. She also incorporated canvas accents along the perimeter of the print.

MY BABY: by Jen Lessinger
Supplies *Photo turn:* 7gypsies; *Canvas paper:* Fredrix; *Heart punch:* EK Success; *Brad:* Creative Imaginations; *Computer fonts:* Dirty Ego, downloaded from the Internet; Century Gothic, Microsoft Word.

FOUR DAYS IN BOSTON: by Erin Lincoln

Supplies *Patterned papers:* KI Memories and Chatterbox; *Photo turns:* 7gypsies; *Metal numbers:* Scrapworks; *Stamping ink:* Dr. Ph. Martin's, Salis International Inc.; *Embossing powder:* Creative Beginnings; *Computer fonts:* CK Regal, "Special Occasions" CD, *Creating Keepsakes;* 2Peas Tasklist, downloaded from *www.twopeasinabucket.com.*

Color Enhanced Photographs

Notice how Erin incorporated color on her pages—she painted a one-inch strip of craft paint over the top of black-and-white photographs and allowed the ink to dry overnight. You can create a similar look on your next page with the following techniques:

• Don't want to paint on your photographs? Paint colored rectangles onto clear transparencies. Cut transparencies and layer them over your photographs.

• Draw image boxes in your favorite publishing program. Fill boxes with color. Print colored boxes onto transparencies and then layer the transparencies over photographs.

• Start with colored transparencies. Cut transparencies into rectangle shapes and layer over the tops of your photographs.

Note: *Look how Erin repeated her colors in her journaling. Each color strip coordinates with a section of journaling. Notice that for Day 2, she painted an orange color strip across the photo and also used orange ink for her journaling.*

"AN AIRPORT AROUND 10:00 AM • FIND A HOTEL• REALIZE PARKING IS EXPENSIVE

LAND AT LOGAN AIRPORT AROUND 10:00 AM • FIND RENTAL CAR AND HOTEL• REALIZE PARKING IS EXPENSIVE GO FANEUIL HALL AND EAT • WALK PART OF THE FREEDOM TRAIL • RIDE THE SWAN BOATS • GET LOST GOING TO "THE NO NAME" RESTAURANT• LONG WALK BACK TO HOTEL

index